Grades 2–3

Art Projects That Dazzle & Delight

BY **Karen Backus**, **Linda Evans**, **Mary Thompson**, AND **Karen Trush**

SCHOLASTIC
PROFESSIONAL BOOKS

NEW YORK • TORONTO • LONDON • AUCKLAND • SYDNEY
MEXICO CITY • NEW DELHI • HONG KONG • BUENOS AIRES

This book is dedicated to all those "children at heart"
who have inspired us to teach.

Thank you,
Karen Backus, Linda Evans,
Mary Thompson, and Karen Trush

Interior illustrations by James Graham Hale
Front cover and interior design by Kathy Massaro

ISBN: 0-439-15388-3

Contents

Introduction

This book grew from a workshop titled Fabulous Projects for Elementary Art, which we presented in 1998 at the New York State Art Teachers Conference in Albany, New York. Using ideas from our presentation, as well as many from our current classes, we have compiled workable and easy-to-manage art activities that will enhance your classroom and help students develop an appreciation for the arts.

The lessons follow a step-by-step format and help students focus on the building blocks of art concepts and vocabulary. The projects include a wide variety of techniques and materials. Using both imagination and creativity, the possibilities are endless. We hope you will enjoy sharing these hands-on activities with your class.

Helpful Hints

Preparation

🎨 A few steps of preparation can prevent disasters. In advance, plan the cleanup procedure for each project. Children love to help, and with a little direction, you'll have a quick and effective cleanup.

🎨 In advance, gather supplies and cut paper to the size specified for each activity. (The paper size does not need to be exact.)

🎨 Always try an art project yourself before presenting it to students. Your experience will serve you well in anticipating any problems that might arise.

🎨 When students are going to cut something along the fold of a folded piece of paper, have them first mark the folded edge with an X. When it's time to cut, tell students to "hold the fold."

To save time, paper, and erasers, first have students practice drawing a shape with a finger on the paper or in the air. This step lets you check for understanding and offer help in working out potential problems.

Paint smocks are the best insurance for hassle-free painting. Men's short-sleeved T-shirts or button-down shirts worn backward offer great coverage.

If the artwork needs to dry, plan ahead for a place to put it. A clothesline and clothespins may work where space is limited.

If students are easily distracted or are eager to begin and don't wait for directions, distribute the art supplies on an "as needed" basis.

If a project calls for a certain mood, plan to play music that is related to the activity.

Before students begin a project, have them write their names on the back of their paper.

Introducing a Project

Whenever possible, show students photographs, drawings, or other visuals that relate to each project. For example, display photographs of owls to introduce Collage Owls (pages 46–48) and prints of Impressionist paintings to introduce Mountain Majesty (pages 10–12). Suggestions are presented throughout the book.

Introduce children to artistic terms that may be unfamiliar to them. For each activity, you'll find a short list of words that will be helpful for children to know as they complete the activity. These words are highlighted the first time they appear in the activity.

In the sections entitled "Let's Begin," you'll find suggested ways to introduce each project.

Drawing

Many lessons in this book refer to the "look and draw" technique. This is a step-by-step method of drawing that works well with young students. The object is not to have students' art be a copy of yours but rather to help them succeed in executing the activities. This method is especially useful in assisting students in positioning objects in particular places on their paper.

When using this method, position yourself in a spot that allows the class a clear view. Draw a few lines at a time, have students observe, and then have them follow your example. Keep in mind that the beauty of children's artwork lies in their unique way of seeing the world. Look for ways to encourage their originality and to help them express their ideas.

🎨 Encourage students always to try! Sharing your own struggles may make some students feel more at ease when attempting something new.

Painting

🎨 Put tempera paints on foam trays or paper plates for easy cleanup.

🎨 Use garbage bags to cover work surfaces. Cut off the bottom of a bag and slit one side, then tape it to the sides of a table. You can wipe off the garbage bag cover and reuse it if desired.

🎨 To clean tempera paint off paintbrushes, soak the brushes for ten minutes in water with a little dishwashing soap. The paint will rinse off quickly.

Displaying Students' Work

🎨 How artwork is displayed can make the difference between "so-so" and "wow!" viewer responses. You'll find specific suggestions for displaying each of the projects in this book. Try out your own ideas, and encourage students to contribute theirs as well.

🎨 A simple way to mount artwork starts with a little planning. For a painting activity, give students paper that has been trimmed an inch on each side. For example, cut a 12- by 18-inch sheet of paper so that it's 11 inches by 17 inches. You can then glue the painting onto the larger sheet to create a border.

🎨 Use large background paper to unify your displays and help avoid the distraction of wall color or patterns.

Watercolor Landscapes

Students use watercolor techniques to create a country landscape.

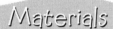
Materials

- landscape photographs
- 9- by 12-inch heavy white paper
- pencils
- soft-bristle paintbrushes
- water containers
- watercolor paints
- crayons
- markers
- brightly colored or black paper (optional, for mounting)

New Art Words

landscape
horizon line
background
middle ground
foreground
wash of color
wet on wet

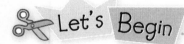
Let's Begin

Display photographs or paintings of country **landscapes** (found in magazines or on calendars). Point out that landscapes are also the subject of many paintings. Tell students that they too will be making landscape paintings in this project.

Pass out the materials. Then demonstrate the following procedures as children follow along.

Step by Step

1 Place a sheet of white paper in a horizontal position. Estimate about one-third of the way down from the top of the paper, and draw a flowing pencil line to create an interesting **horizon line** (the point at which the sky and land meet). As you draw, explain that an artist uses color, size, and placement of objects to give the feeling of space.

2 Draw a second line below the horizon line to create the **background** space for painting. Continue to divide the space from left to right to create the **middle ground** and **foreground**.

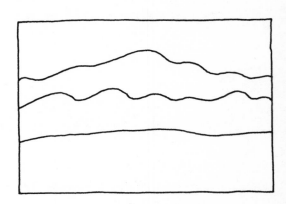

3 Use simple geometric shapes to sketch trees, fences, barns, and roads. Point out that larger images should be placed in the foreground and that smaller images should be placed in the background. This helps to create an illusion of depth.

～ Tip ～

Tell students that they can create cloud formations by leaving areas of the sky unpainted.

4 Demonstrate the painting process. Stress that this step is most successful if you paint an area rapidly and then leave it to dry. To paint the sky, begin with a clean, wet brush. Apply water to the top section of the paper (sky). Wet the watercolor paints and load the brush with paint to apply a **wash of color**. As wet paint comes into contact with water on the paper's surface, it will explode into exciting designs. Explain that this process is called **wet on wet**. Model this for students by letting purple paint "run" across the top of the painting. Do not brush over the color; allow the water to create the images.

5 Explain that cool colors (blue, green, and violet) used in the background appear to recede. Apply a light wash of color to suggest a background, using a small amount of paint and a lot of water. Gradually add more color to the middle ground and complete the foreground with the strongest wash of color. Allow the painting to dry before adding details in the next step.

6 Dry brushstrokes (very little water and a stiffer brush) add texture to a watercolor painting. Drag the brush to create grass or tree foliage. Have students paint in details or use a crayon on its side to create a more textured look. Suggest that students use a marker to outline fences and indicate farm fields.

One Step More

Encourage students to select local landmarks as the subject of their next landscape painting. Can the rest of the class identify these local places from the paintings?

Bookshelf

Grandma Moses by Tom Biracree (Chelsea House, 1989)

Morgan and the Artist by Donald Carrick (Clarion Books, 1985)

Places in Art by Anthea Peppin (Millbrook Press, 1992)

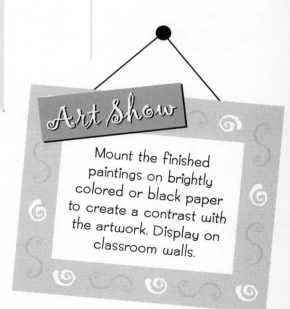

Art Show

Mount the finished paintings on brightly colored or black paper to create a contrast with the artwork. Display on classroom walls.

Mountain Majesty

**Students mix tempera paints to
experiment with color and create
a mountain scene.**

Materials

- examples of Impressionist paintings by Monet, Van Gogh, and others (greeting cards, postcards, and calendars are excellent sources)
- 12- by 18-inch heavy white paper
- pencils
- tempera paint (yellow, blue, white, and purple)
- paintbrushes
- 8-inch paper plates (for palettes)
- water containers

New Art Words

movement
palette
foreground
middle ground
background

Let's Begin

Discuss examples of Impressionist paintings. Draw attention to the way the paint is applied with large brushstrokes. Point out that swirling or dabbing brushstrokes create a feeling of **movement**, and while the colors may not be realistic, they, too, invoke feelings. Have students notice the use of warm colors (red, yellow, and orange) for a hot summer day or cool colors (blue, purple, and green) for a nighttime scene. Explain that an artist uses a **palette** to mix different colors of paint.

Cover work surfaces to prepare for painting, and pass out the materials. Then demonstrate the following procedures as children follow along.

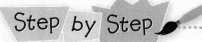 Step by Step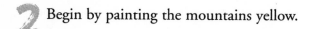

1 Place a sheet of paper in a horizontal position. In the middle of the paper, draw a slightly curved line to indicate the base of mountains. Next, sketch gentle, curving lines for the mountains. Overlap the mountains to create a feeling of depth. Explain that at this point you have determined the three areas of the landscape: the **foreground** (the area closest to the bottom of the page, in front of the mountains), the **middle ground** (the mountains), and the **background** (the sky).

2 Begin by painting the mountains yellow.

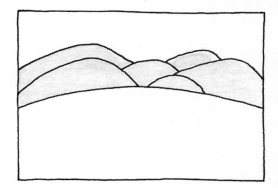

3 Tell students that you will create three different shades of green paint by mixing varying amounts of yellow and blue. Encourage students to mix colors in small areas on their paper-plate palette so they will have space to mix many colors. Select three areas and dab a small amount of yellow in each spot. Then add the blue paint a little at a time to create three shades of green.

4 Use the three shades of green paint in large, overlapping strokes for the grass. (This is a good point to stop; complete the next steps in a second session.)

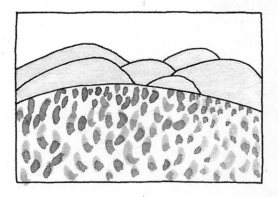

5 Use blue and white paints for the sky. Mix colors on the palette, and apply the paint in a swirling motion to indicate movement in the clouds and changing weather.

6 Use purple paint to outline the contour of the mountains.

One Step More

Use crayons to create a night scene of the same landscape. Make lines with the crayons in the same way you did with paints: swirly lines for the night sky, large strokes of color for the grass, and smooth, blended colors for the mountains.

Bookshelf

Camille and the Sunflowers: A Story About Vincent Van Gogh by Laurence Anholt (Barron's Educational Series, 1994)

Katie Meets the Impressionists by James Mayhew (Orchard Books, 1999)

The Starry Night by Neil Waldman (Boyds Mills Press, 1999)

Van Gogh by Mike Venezia (Children's Press, 1988)

Van Gogh: Famous Artist by Andrew S. Hughes (Barron's Educational Series, 1994)

Art Show

Display students' paintings alongside examples of Impressionist landscapes.

Cardboard City

Students collaborate to create colorful city buildings out of cardboard.

Materials

- pictures of city buildings
- cardboard cut into various lengths and widths (empty fabric bolts work well)
- tempera paint (various colors)
- paintbrushes
- water containers
- 1- by 12-inch strips of yellow and white construction paper
- scissors
- glue
- construction paper (various colors and sizes to be used for architectural details)
- markers or crayons

New Art Words

architecture
skyscraper
geometric shapes
symmetrical
accordion fold

Let's Begin

Display pictures of various types of buildings that are found in a city. Discuss the different types of **architecture**. Introduce the word **skyscraper**. Draw attention to the **geometric shapes** found in different buildings. Point out that most windows are **symmetrical**. Explain that students will work together to make a cardboard city that consists of different types of buildings.

Cover the work surfaces with newspaper, and pass out the materials. Then demonstrate the following procedures.

Step by Step

1 Discuss the different colors and types of building materials. Ask students which colors might be used to represent various building materials. For example, red might be used to represent a brick building, brown for wood, gray for concrete, or white for stucco.

2 Have students choose a color and paint a piece of cardboard. Set aside the cardboard to dry.

3 To create windows, take a strip of white or yellow construction paper and fold it back and forth in the shape of a square or rectangle. Explain that this is an **accordion fold**. Cut along the fold lines to make small squares or rectangles.

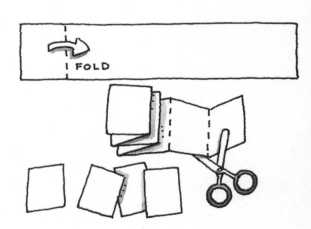

4 Glue the squares and rectangles in vertical rows on the dry cardboard to create windows. Use a larger rectangle for the door.

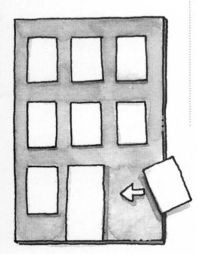

5 Cut curtains and signs from various colors of construction paper. Add details (folds in curtains, words on the signs), using markers or crayons.

6 Cut slits in two rectangular pieces of cardboard. Place these pieces on the bottom of each building to hold it upright.

One Step More

Students might use construction paper to create details such as trees and sidewalks to add to the cityscape.

Art Show

Assemble the buildings on one or more "streets" to create an interesting skyline. Invite guests to your classroom to visit your city.

Bookshelf

Piero Ventura's Book of Cities by Piero Ventura
    (Random House, 1975)

Round Buildings, Square Buildings by Philip Isaacson
    (Knopf, 1988)

Round Trip by Ann Jonas (Greenwillow Books, 1983)

Reflecting Line Designs

This project combines art, math, and science skills.

Materials

- pictures of reflections
- mirror
- 10- by 16-inch heavy white paper
- pencils
- tempera paint (various colors)
- paintbrushes
- water containers
- 12- by 18-inch black paper (optional, for mounting)

New Art Words

reflection

horizontal

pattern

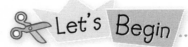 **Let's Begin**

Show students several pictures of **reflections**, in mirrors and in water. Point out that the objects reflected are upside down in the water and reversed in the mirrors. Explain that students will be creating a "water" reflection, with the lines upside down or opposite each other.

Pass out the materials. Then demonstrate the following procedures as children follow along.

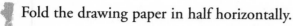

Step by Step

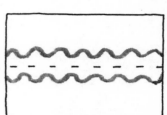

FOLD

1 Fold the drawing paper in half horizontally.

2 Open the folded paper. Instruct students to draw a simple curved **horizontal** line just above the center fold of the paper.

3 A little below the center of the paper, create another line that reflects the first one. In other words, the second line is the same as the first but is drawn upside down, as if seen in water.

4 Direct students to continue making line designs above and below the first two lines. Each line should reflect, or be the opposite of, the initial design in each pair, creating a reverse image.

5 Continue in this manner until the paper is filled with horizontal reflecting lines.

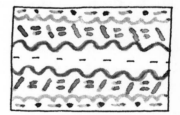

6 Have students paint their lines in "reflecting" colors. For example, if there is a blue line painted on the top, have them paint a matching blue line in the reflected design.

One Step More

Suggest that students add two or three details to the **patterns**. Remind students that a pattern is a design that is repeated.

Bookshelf

Pattern by Kim Taylor (Belitha Press, 1993)

Reflections by Ann Jonas (William Morrow, 1987)

Shadows and Reflections by Tana Hoban (Greenwillow Press, 1990)

Art Show

Mount the finished reflection paintings on sheets of black paper, and display with several photographs of reflections.

Patchwork Pets

Using watercolor and crayons, students explore color and design to make fanciful patchwork cats.

Materials

- examples of line designs
- reproductions of art featuring animals
- 12- by 18-inch heavy white paper
- pencils
- black crayons
- watercolor paints
- small paintbrushes
- water containers
- scissors
- glue
- 12- by 18-inch colored construction paper

New Art Words

diagonal

rhythm

variety

pattern

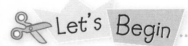 Let's Begin

Display a variety of designs that are made with lines. Examples include zigzags, swirls, waves, stripes, and checks. Encourage students to look for repeating designs on their clothing.

Show students examples of different styles of artwork depicting animals. Discuss the differences between a realistic rendering of a cat, a photograph, an abstract picture, and a cartoon. Tell students that they will create their own cats by making a patchwork of line designs.

Pass out the materials. Then demonstrate the following procedures as children follow along.

Step by Step

1 Place a sheet of white paper in a vertical position. Use the look-and-draw method (children observe while you draw, then they draw) to draw a pencil outline of a seated cat. Near the top of the paper, draw a round shape for the head. Draw two triangles at the top of the circle for ears.

2 Draw eyes in the shape of a football. Draw a downward-pointing triangle for the nose. Begin the line for the mouth at the point of the nose. Draw the shape of a fishhook going one way and then the other.

3 Draw an oval for the cat's body. Add a tail, either curved up or on the ground. Make the tail wide enough to be easily cut out (students can measure a width of at least two fingers). Draw the two front feet by making two large *U* shapes.

4 Using a black crayon, apply heavy pressure as you carefully trace the pencil outline of the cat. To make the patchwork sections for the designs, draw **diagonal** lines inside the cat's body. Begin by drawing a diagonal line from the top of the cat's back to the opposite side. This may create a large or small area; any size will work. Add additional diagonal lines, beginning at any spot on the cat, until six or seven sections have been created.

5 Instruct students to use a crayon to draw a different line design for each section of their cat. Explain that the objective is to create **rhythm** and **variety** by filling each space with a different **pattern**.

6 Have students paint each section of the cat a different color.

7 When the paint is dry, carefully cut out the cats and glue them onto brightly colored construction paper.

Tip

Remind students that watercolors will run together when wet. Unless this effect is desired, have students paint shapes that are not touching to eliminate unwanted mixing of the colors.

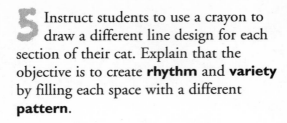

One Step More

Students might use crayons or markers to add a background. They might also choose to place the animal in the wild, in a cage, or as a toy on a shelf.

Art Show

Display the patchwork cats with patterned fabric samples, stuffed animals, or as a crazy quilt.

Bookshelf

A Bad Case of Stripes by David Shannon (Blue Sky Press, 1998)

Elmer by David McKee (Lothrop, Lee & Shepard, 1989, © 1968)

Artful Alphabet

Students use a letter of the alphabet as the basis for a design that shows an animal in its habitat.

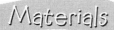
Materials

- pictures of animals in various habitats
- enlarged copies of letter patterns (pages 23–24)
- 12- by 18-inch white paper
- pencils
- markers
- scissors
- scraps of colored paper
- glue
- 12- by 18-inch colored paper (optional, for mounting)

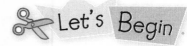
Let's Begin

Display pictures of various animals. Write the alphabet on the chalkboard, and brainstorm a list of animal names that start with each letter. Ask students to select an animal and think about how that animal could fit within the shape of the letter that begins its name.

Make copies of the **block letters** on pages 23–24, and provide students with enlargements of the letter they will need. For example, a student who chooses to create a kangaroo will need an enlarged letter *K*. Pass out the other materials. Then demonstrate the following procedures as children follow along.

Step by Step

1 Using the white paper and pencil, trace the block letter *F* so that it touches the sides of the paper.

2 Draw an outline of a fish to fit inside the shape of the letter. Explain that students may need to **exaggerate**, stretch, or bend their animals so that they conform to the shape of the letter. Students can also use their animals to form part of the letter, as shown in the illustration of the fish and *F*.

3 Use markers to highlight details such as scales, fur, and other animal markings. Cut out the letter.

4 Using scraps of colored paper, cut out wavy shapes to represent the sea. You can cut **repeating patterns** from folded paper to save time. Discuss with students shapes they might cut out for their animal habitats, such as circles for stones or triangles for trees.

5 Glue the habitat shapes onto the letters. Be sure students understand that they don't have to cover the entire letter.

One Step More

Use the alphabet to illustrate new themes such as favorite foods, musical instruments, or flowers and plants.

Art Show

Mount the letters on colored paper. Display them in alphabetical order with an alliterative description for each, such as, "Friendly fish find floating fun."

Bookshelf

Animal Action by Karen Pandell and Art Wolfe (Dutton, 1996)

Bugs and Beasties ABC by Cheryl Nathan (Cool Kids Press, 1995)

On Market Street by Anita Lobel (Greenwillow Books, 1981)

Tomorrow's Alphabet by George Shannon (Greenwillow Books, 1995)

Letter Patterns

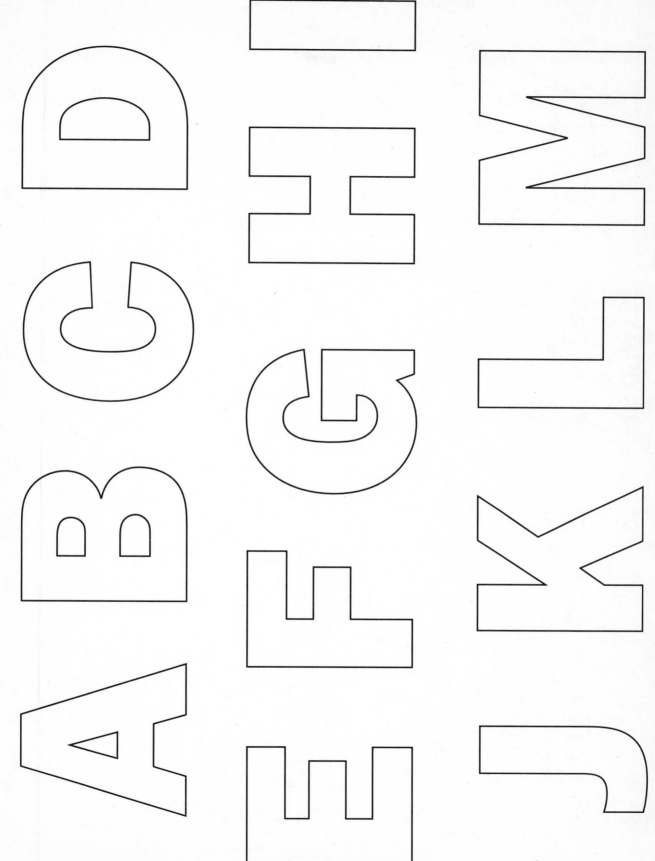

Art Projects That Dazzle & Delight (Grades 2–3) Scholastic Professional Books

Teatime

Students use a variety of lines to draw and paint a teapot with a three-dimensional quality.

Materials

- teapots or photographs of teapots
- 9- by 12-inch light-colored heavy paper (for teapot)
- pencils
- tempera paint
- paintbrushes
- water containers
- markers
- scissors
- glue
- 9- by 12-inch colored paper (for background)
- paper fasteners

New Art Word

three-dimensional

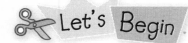

Let's Begin

Have students observe the shapes of teapots. Identify the parts: foot, lid, handle, and spout. Look for fanciful designs on painted teapots. Explain that students will make a drawing of a teapot that gives the illusion of a **three-dimensional** object.

Pass out the materials. Then demonstrate the following procedures as children follow along.

Step by Step

1 Draw two smilelike lines to illustrate the top and bottom curves of the teapot, as shown.

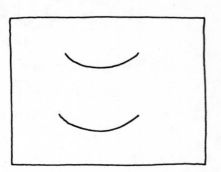

2 Draw rounded lines to complete the sides of the teapot. Top the teapot with an umbrella shape for the lid. Draw a circle at the top of the lid for a knob.

3 Add another curved line to the base to create the foot of the teapot. The curved lines help to create a three-dimensional appearance.

4 Draw double lines for both the handle and spout. Draw an oval at the end of the spout. Explain that it looks as though you can see the inside of the spout when you draw an oval at the tip.

5 Add designs to the teapot, using repeated patterns and ornamentation.

6 Paint the teapot and let it dry.

7 Use markers to outline the designs and add finer details.

8 Cut out the teapot. Cut along the curved line of the lid to make a separate piece.

9 Glue the bottom of the teapot onto a colored strip of paper to suggest a tablecloth. Use markers to draw patterns on the tablecloth. Glue the tablecloth and teapot (but not the teapot lid) onto a contrasting sheet of background paper.

10 Use a paper fastener to attach the lid to the background. Students can gently open and close the lid.

One Step More

Use real fabric for the tablecloth instead of paper.

Art Show

Display the projects, and invite students' families in for a tea party. Pour real tea from real teapots, and have children sing "I'm a Little Teapot."

Bookshelf

The Eccentric Teapot: Four Hundred Years of Invention by Garth Clark (Abbeville Press, 1989)

I'm a Little Teapot by Iza Trapini and Judy Fine (Whispering Coyote Press, 1999)

Teapots: The Collector's Guide by Tina Carter (Book Sales, 1998)

Radial Designs

As they listen to music, students create a radial design painting inspired by natural and manufactured objects.

Materials

- photos of objects with radial designs (orange slices, bicycle wheels, stained glass rose windows, umbrellas)
- newspaper
- tempera paint (red, orange, yellow, green, blue, and violet) or markers
- water containers
- paintbrushes (various sizes)
- 12- by 12-inch heavy white paper
- cassette tapes (various styles of music)
- 14- by 14-inch black or brightly colored paper (optional, for mounting)

New Art Words

radiate

radial patterns

spectrum

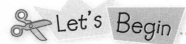 Let's Begin

Show students the radial design photographs and point out how the designs begin in the center and **radiate** to the edges, like the spokes of a bicycle wheel. Tell students to share other examples of **radial patterns**. Inform students that in this activity they will use six colors of the **spectrum**, and that they will begin to paint when the music begins and stop painting when the music stops.

Divide the class into six groups. Cover six work surfaces with newspaper. Distribute one paint color and several different sizes of paintbrushes to each group. You can also substitute markers for the tempera paints.

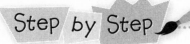

Step by Step

1 Demonstrate how to begin painting in the center of the paper, making a small circular design.

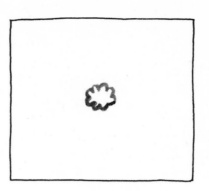

2 Play the music, and have students use their assigned color of paint to paint a design that reflects the pattern of the music.

3 Stop the music and direct groups to change color stations, taking their paintings with them. (Be sure that the paint and brushes stay at the painting stations.)

4 When you start the music again, have students continue their design at the next station, adding to the pattern and making sure that it progresses evenly from the center to the outer edges. You may wish to model the process each time students add another color and pattern to their designs.

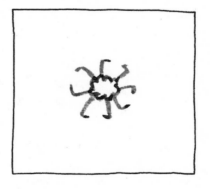

5 Continue in this manner so that students enlarge the radial patterns with each new color. The painting time will vary as each color is added and the painted area increases in size. Students should use all six colors.

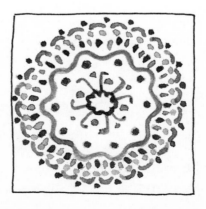

Tip

To help keep shirtsleeves clean, have students turn the paper as their painting progresses.

6 As students reach the outer edge of the paper, they may want to add line designs of a new color to existing patterns.

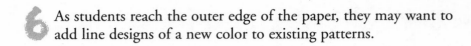
One Step More

When the paintings are dry, have students discuss the success of their work in radial patterning. Ask: "How did the music affect your work?"

Art Show

Mount the paintings on sheets of black or colored paper. Display them, along with photographs or other images of radial designs.

Bookshelf

Lots and Lots of Zebra Stripes: Patterns in Nature by Stephen R. Swinburne (Boyds Mills Press, 1998)

Nature's Paintbrush: The Patterns and Colors Around You by Susan Stockdale (Simon & Schuster, 1999)

Pattern by Henry Pluckrose (Children's Press, 1995)

Pattern: Flying Start Science by Kim Taylor (John Wiley, 1992)

Leaves in Relief

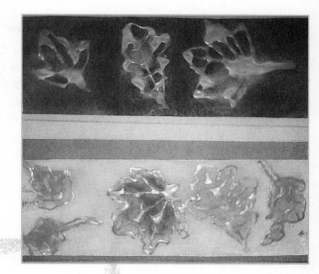

**Students observe nature
and create colorful leaves
using glue and chalk.**

Materials

- pictures of leaves
- collection of real leaves
- leaf patterns (pages 34–35)
- scissors
- 6- by 16-inch construction paper (various colors)
- pencils
- white glue (in squeeze bottles)
- colored chalk
- paper towels
- 8- by 18-inch colored construction paper (optional, for mounting)

New Art Words

overlap

composition

relief

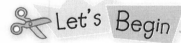 Let's Begin

Discuss various types of leaves and how their shapes differ. Explain that leaves on trees **overlap** one another. Draw students' attention to the colors that can be found in a single leaf. Have students touch the real leaves to feel the raised veins. Note that the color of the veins differs from that of the leaf.

Reproduce and cut out the leaf patterns on pages 34–35 (four patterns per child). Pass out the other materials. Then demonstrate the following procedures.

Step by Step

1 Select a sheet of construction paper. Arrange several leaf patterns on the paper to obtain a well-balanced **composition**. Trace the leaf patterns onto the paper. (Some children will be able to get only three leaves on their paper; others may fit several more.)

2 Draw veins and stems on the leaves.

3 Squeeze the glue over the pencil lines of the leaves.

4 Lay the leaf designs flat to dry overnight. When dry, the glue lines will feel raised to the touch, creating a **relief**.

5 Use colored chalk to fill in the areas between the glue lines. Chalk may be blended using two or more colors. Apply a small amount of chalk in each section and rub gently with a finger or paper towel. (NOTE: The blending of too many colors will result in a muddy brown leaf.) If the paper you are using is a light color such as yellow, use blue or purple chalk. Yellow and orange chalk work best with dark-colored paper such as green or blue.

6 When the leaves are complete, choose a new color of chalk and color the background.

◌◟ Tip ◞◌

To get the best results, the glue line should be the width of thick spaghetti. If the glue separates, reapply to establish a continuous line.

One Step More

Add to the leaves a worm or bug created from paper. Mount the finished projects on colored construction paper.

Bookshelf

Autumn Leaves by Ken Robbins
    (Scholastic, 1998)

Look What I Did With a Leaf
    by Morteza E. Sohi (Walker, 1993)

Red Leaf, Yellow Leaf by Lois Ehlert
    (Harcourt Brace, 1991)

Why Do Leaves Change Color?
    by Betsy Maestro (HarperCollins, 1994)

Art Show

Display the chalk-and-glue leaves with an explanation of the creative process. Add stems of real leaves to enhance your display.

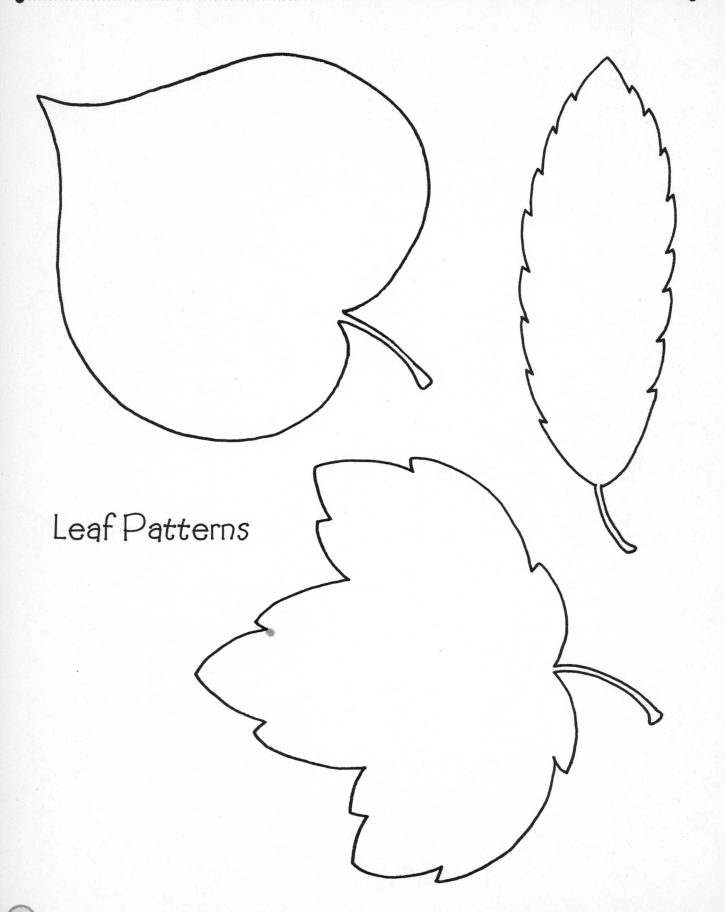

Leaf Patterns

Art Projects That Dazzle & Delight: Grades 2–3 Scholastic Professional Books

Leaf Patterns

In the Wild

This activity combines art and science as students draw and paint a wild animal in its habitat.

Materials

- pictures of various animals in their habitats
- pencils
- 11- by 11-inch heavy white paper
- black crayons
- watercolor paints
- paintbrushes
- water containers
- 15- by 15-inch black construction paper
- glue
- 2- by 11-inch paper strips
- crayons or markers

New Art Words

texture

composition

overlapping

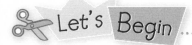

Let's Begin

Display pictures of various animals in their habitats. Discuss the types of environments and why certain animals live where they do. Draw attention to the **textures** of different animals. Have students choose an animal they would like to draw in its habitat. Discuss how they would begin to create a well-balanced **composition**.

Pass out the materials. Then demonstrate the following procedures as children follow along.

Step by Step

1 Using pencil on white paper, draw an animal (look at the pictures for reference). Remind students to draw their animal large enough to fill a good portion of the paper, leaving some area for its habitat.

2 Add details such as fur, feathers, spots, stripes, and so on, to indicate the animal's texture and pattern.

3 Draw the animal's habitat in the remaining area. To make the animal appear to be peeking out, encourage the **overlapping** of leaves and trees.

4 Trace over the pencil drawing with black crayon.

5 Use watercolors to paint the animals, and then set the paintings aside to dry.

6 Mount the animal paintings on black construction paper.

One Step More

Have students design a border using footprints of the animal in their painting. Draw the footprints on a strip of foam from a meat tray. Trace over the footprints with a dull pencil to indent them. Roll over the foam with tempera paint on a brayer or foam roller. To print, press onto four strips of paper and glue the strips onto the mounting paper.

Bookshelf

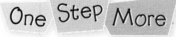

Footprints in the Snow by Cynthia Benjamin
(Scholastic, 1994)

***Too Many Rabbits and Other Fingerplays About
Animals, Nature, Weather, and the Universe***
by Kay Cooper (Scholastic, 1995)

Art Show

Display the paintings along with a list of all the animals portrayed. Invite students to match the animal names with the correct paintings.

Leaves on a Limb

This activity combines representational drawing, leaf printing, and collage techniques.

Materials

- various leaves and branches
- 8- by 16-inch white drawing paper
- 12- by 20-inch mounting paper in warm colors (red, yellow, and orange)
- white glue
- pencils
- fine-point black markers
- tempera paint (brown, yellow, red, and orange)
- paper plates
- easel brushes
- water containers
- paper towels

New Art Words

contour

realistic

print

composition

Let's Begin

Fall is the perfect time to explore various types of leaves. Begin by passing out the leaves, one to each student. Help students discover what makes each leaf unique. Have them use their fingers to trace around the edge of the leaf, noticing all the ins and outs of each leaf. Explain that students will create leaves in three different ways—by drawing, printing, and making collages.

Mount the drawing paper on warm-colored paper. Pass out the paper and pencils. Then demonstrate the following procedures.

Step by Step

1 Place a branch where students can easily view it. Then begin drawing the branch, using a **contour** line. Instruct them to look very carefully at the edges of the branch and to draw very slowly. Tell them to let their eyes follow the contour, or edge, of the branch. Students should attempt to make a **realistic**, or exact, drawing of the branch. If desired, extend the drawing onto the mounting paper.

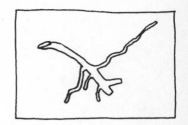

2 Next, add one or more leaves to the drawing, continuing to draw slowly with contour lines.

3 Trace over the drawing with a fine-point marker.

4 Distribute easel brushes and paper plates with tempera paint. Provide a leaf for each student, and explain that students will paint the back, or underside, of the leaf with one or more colors. Students will then turn their leaf over and press it onto their branch drawing. Place a folded paper towel over the leaf and press with one hand to **print**.

5 Glue a natural unpainted leaf onto the branch to complete the **composition**, or layout, of the leaves.

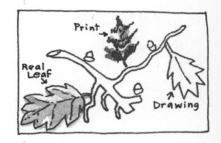

One Step More

Students may wish to draw or print more than one leaf. Encourage them to create a pleasing composition. Students can make interesting colors by applying two colors to the leaf before printing. If students use oak leaves, they might add acorns to the composition.

Bookshelf

Autumn Leaves by Ken Robbins (Scholastic Press, 1998)

The Fall of Freddie the Leaf by Leo Buscaglia (Holt, 1982)

Look What I Did With a Leaf by Morteza E. Sohi (Walker, 1993)

The Tiny Seed by Eric Carle (Crowell, 1970)

Art Show

Use students' artwork to decorate your classroom for a fall celebration or as part of a science unit on trees.

Hand-Puppet Birds

In this imaginative activity, students create colorful bird hand puppets.

Materials

- 9- by 18-inch colored construction paper
- 3- by 5-inch yellow paper
- scissors
- glue

- scraps of colored paper
- 1/2- by 12-inch strips of colored paper
- pencils

New Art Words

lengthwise

curl

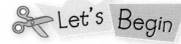 Let's Begin ··

Ask students if they have ever heard a talking bird. Explain that some birds, such as parrots, can learn words. Then tell the class that they will be making their own talking birds in this activity; these birds will be paper puppets.

Pass out the materials. Then demonstrate the following procedures as children follow along.

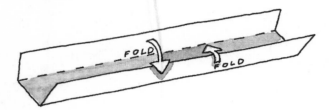

Step by Step

1 Fold a sheet of colored construction paper into thirds **lengthwise**. Flip over the paper and fold in half as shown.

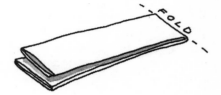

2 Fold the bottom edge back to meet the fold. Then fold the top edge back to meet the fold. Fold with open edges to the outside. This will create pockets for fingers.

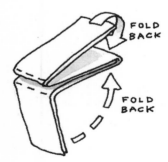

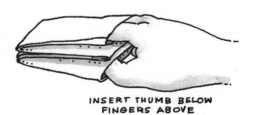

INSERT THUMB BELOW
FINGERS ABOVE

3 To form a beak, cut triangles out of two pieces of yellow paper. Fold lengthwise to help give the beak dimension. Glue the corners of the beak onto the top and bottom edges of the paper folded in steps 1 and 2. If desired, glue a small tongue onto the inside bottom of the beak.

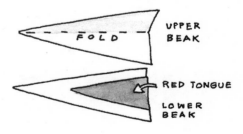

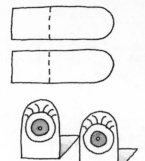

4 From paper scraps, cut two *U*-shaped eyes. Fold the straight edge of each eye and glue on as a pop-up. Add paper circles for eyeballs. If desired, draw imaginative details.

5 Use paper strips for the feathers. **Curl** the ends over a pencil and glue onto the top of the bird's head. Let the glue dry.

WRAP PAPER AROUND PENCIL

GLUE

6 Place your fingers inside the top slot of the paper and your thumb inside the bottom slot to make your bird puppet "talk."

One Step More

Have students write a short biographical introduction about their bird puppet that they can present to the class.

Art Show

To make a puppet theater, cut a window out of a large cardboard box or drape a sheet over a clothesline. Invite children to perform.

Bookshelf

Hand Puppets: How to Make and Use Them by Laura Ross (Lothrop, Lee & Shepard, 1969)

Making Puppets Come Alive: How to Learn and Teach Hand Puppetry by Larry Engler (Taplinger, 1973)

Tropical Birds

Enhance classroom studies of the rain forest with this paint-a-parrot project.

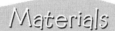
Materials

- pictures of macaws
- 12- by 18-inch white drawing paper
- pencils
- tempera paint (black, red, blue, and yellow)
- paintbrushes (various sizes)
- 4- by 12-inch strips of red, blue, and yellow construction paper
- scissors
- glue or stapler
- scraps of black and brown construction paper

New Art Words

primary colors

outline

fringe

three-dimensional

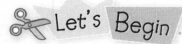
Let's Begin

It would be almost impossible to study the rain forest without discovering some of the beautiful tropical birds that live in it. Macaws are a tropical bird that most children have seen on TV or at the zoo. Explain to students that they will be drawing a large macaw and outlining it in black paint. Use pictures of macaws for reference.

Set up three work stations with large paintbrushes and a **primary color** paint at each (red, blue, and yellow). Pass out the other materials. Then demonstrate the following procedures.

Step by Step

1 Guide students through the look-and-draw method to create their macaw with pencil on white paper. Encourage them to fill the whole paper. Begin with a partial circle at the top of the paper for a head.

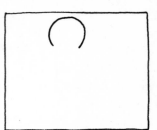

2 Draw an oval body shape below the head.

3 Add the eyes, beak, and feathers. Explain that the beak is a hook shape, and the feather layers are a series of curved lines drawn across the body.

4 After the drawing is complete, have students **outline**, or paint over all the lines, with black tempera paint and a small brush. Let dry.

5 Show students the primary colors—red, blue, or yellow—at each worktable. Students will move from table to table to paint each section of the bird. (Be sure that the paint and brushes stay at the painting stations.) Guide students to paint within the areas outlined in black, as they would color in a coloring book. Have students continue until the paintings are complete.

6 When the paintings are dry, instruct students to cut out their birds along the outside black line.

7 To make the tail feathers, each student will need three or four strips of colored paper. Have students trim both ends to a point, like a feather.

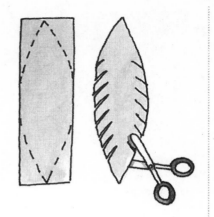

8 Make small cuts along both sides of the feather to create **fringe**, and fold or bend the edges to give a **three-dimensional** feathered look.

9 Assemble the tail feathers on the macaw, using glue or a stapler to attach them.

One Step More

Students can add feet cut from black construction paper. They can also cut a branch from brown construction paper for the macaw's perch.

Bookshelf

At Home in the Rain Forest by Diane Willow (Charlesbridge, 1991)

Rainforest Birds (Birds Up Close) by Bobbie Kalman (Crabtree, 1998)

A Walk in the Rainforest by Kristen Joy Pratt (Dawn, 1992)

Art Show

These tropical macaws look great perched in a large paper tree or on a branch in the hall. Add paper leaves or real tree branches for a more dramatic display.

Collage Owls

Students will enjoy using cut and torn paper to assemble an owl.

Materials

- ***Owl Moon*** by Jane Yolen (or another owl story)
- 12- by 18-inch construction paper in several shades of brown and tan
- pencils
- scissors
- 9- by 12-inch brown and tan paper
- glue
- 3- by 3-inch squares of yellow paper (2 for each student)
- 1- by 1-inch small black squares (2 per student)
- 1- by 3-inch orange paper (1 per student)
- newspaper
- 12- by 18-inch colored construction paper (optional, for mounting)

New Art Words

symmetrical

overlap

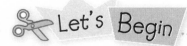 Let's Begin

Introduce the lesson by reading an owl story to the class. (See suggestions under BOOKSHELF.) Discuss different kinds of owls and their characteristics (wings, feathers, claws, eyes, and beak). Invite students to describe owls they have seen in the wild, at zoos, or in photographs.

Pass out the materials. Then demonstrate the following procedures as children follow along.

Step by Step

1 Have students choose a 12- by 18-inch sheet of brown or tan paper. Model how to fold the paper in half vertically.

2 Beginning at the top of the paper and on the fold, guide students as they use the look-and-draw method to create a pencil drawing of the owl's body. Encourage students to use the whole paper so the owl will be large.

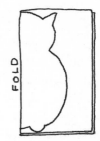

3 Cut out the body, with the paper still folded. The result will be a complete owl body that consists of two **symmetrical** sides.

4 Have students choose a sheet of 9- by 12-inch paper of a different shade of brown or tan. Fold this paper in half, 9-inch side to 9-inch side. Draw a wing as shown, filling the entire page.

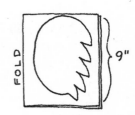

5 Cut out the wings and glue them onto the sides of the owl's body. Draw lines on the feet.

6 For the eyes, cut ovals from yellow paper. Cut a black circle and glue it onto the center of the eye. Glue the eyes onto the owl's head.

7 To make the beak, fold the orange paper rectangle in half so that the shorter edges touch. Make a dot in the center of the open side of the paper. Draw lines to the end of the fold, forming a V. Cut out the beak and glue it onto the owl's head. (**HINT:** Glue only on the fold so the beak will look three-dimensional.)

8 Have students tear a pile of feathers, about two inches in length, from a sheet of newspaper. Instruct students to glue these onto the bottom of the owl's body. Show students how to apply a row of white glue dots and apply several paper feathers at a time. Apply the next layer of glue dots about one inch above the first, and continue to **overlap** the feathers until the body is full.

9 Tear leftover scraps of brown construction paper to make more feathers, and glue them onto the owl's wings and head. Alert students to the fact that what look like ears are really tufts of feathers.

One Step More

When the owls are complete, tape a small tree branch onto the back of the owl behind its feet.

Art Show

Display the owls on large tree branches, or mount them each on a sheet of 12- by 18-inch background paper.

Bookshelf

The Owl and the Pussycat by Edward Lear and Jan Brett (Putnam, 1991)

Owl at Home by Arnold Lobel (HarperTrophy, 1996)

Owl Moon by Jane Yolen (Philomel, 1987)

The Owl Who Couldn't Give a Hoot by Don Conway (Dufour Editions, 1994)

Watercolor
Landscapes

◄

Page 7

Mountain Majesty ►

Page 10

◄ **Cardboard City**

Page 13

Reflecting Line Designs

Page 16

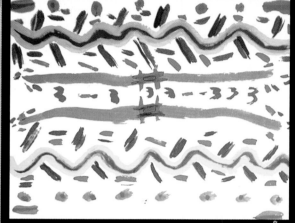

Patchwork Pets

Page 18

Artful Alphabet ▶

Page 21

Tropical Birds ▶

Page 43

◀ Collage Owls

Page 46

Bird Molas ▶

Page 49

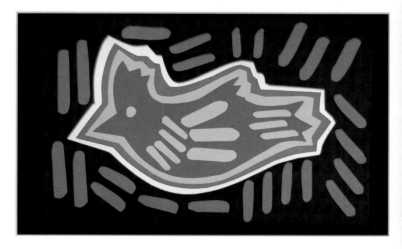

◀ **Self-Portraits**

Page 53

▲ **Friends With Hats**

Page 56

Symmetrical Smiles

Page 58

Carnival Creatures

Page 61

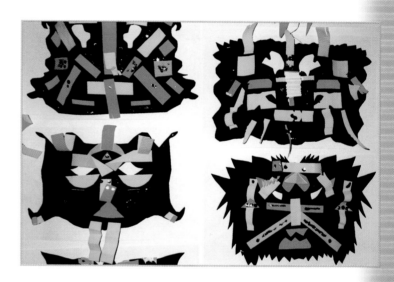

Beach Ball Collage

Page 64

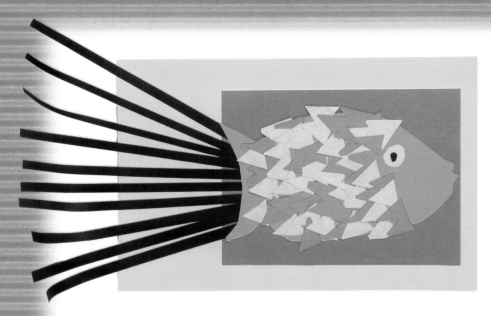

Bird Molas

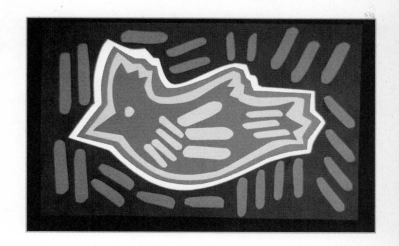

This project combines art with a lesson about cultural awareness.

Materials

- bird patterns (page 52)
- 9- by 12-inch construction paper (various bright colors and black)
- pencils
- scissors
- glue

New Art Words

mola

repeat pattern

enlargement

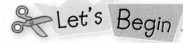 Let's Begin

Explain to students that a **mola** is a folk art design created by the Cuna Indians of Panama. It is a unique craft consisting of layers of fabric that are cut and stitched together to form decorative panels. Geometric patterns and subjects such as fish, birds, and animals are often used in these designs, which consist of layered **repeat patterns**. The word *mola* means "blouse" in the Cuna Indian language. Traditional molas were created on blouses, but today they are often framed as decorative panels of artwork. Tell students that they will create molas out of brightly colored construction paper.

Duplicate the bird patterns on page 52. Pass out the materials. Then demonstrate the following procedures as children follow along.

Step by Step

1 Choose a bird pattern and a sheet of colored construction paper. Cut out the bird pattern. Using a pencil, trace the outline of the bird onto the construction paper. Cut out the bird shape.

2 Glue the bird shape onto the center of another sheet of colored construction paper. Choose complementary colors to create a sharp contrast; for example, red and green, blue and orange, or violet and yellow.

3 With a pencil, draw an **enlargement** of the bird about one finger width around the entire shape, as shown. Cut out the enlarged bird shape. You now have a two-colored bird.

4 Repeat steps 2 and 3 two times, using two additional colors. Your finished bird should have four colors.

5 Glue the bird onto the center of a sheet of black construction paper. Do not cut this paper.

6 Cut narrow stick shapes in various lengths from the construction paper scraps. Glue these onto the bird and black background to form patterns. Glue a paper circle for an eye.

One Step More

Invite students to learn more about molas and the people who create them.

Bookshelf

Cuckoo: A Mexican Folktale by Lois Ehlert
  (Harcourt Brace, 1997)

Musicians of the Sun by Gerald McDermott
  (Simon & Schuster, 1997)

Zomo the Rabbit by Gerald McDermott
  (Harcourt Brace, 1992)

Art Show

Display the artwork along with student reports about the history and background of molas.

Bird Patterns

Self-Portraits

Students learn about facial proportions as they create expressive self-portraits using colored pencils.

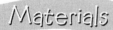 Materials

- examples of self-portraits by artists
- 6- by 6-inch white paper
- hand mirrors (if available)
- pencils
- erasers
- colored pencils
- 8- by 8-inch colored paper, or larger (optional, for mounting)

 New Art Words

facial proportions

symmetrical

shade

blending

overlapping

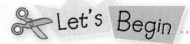 Let's Begin

Look at and discuss examples of self-portraits with the class. Explain that **facial proportions** follow certain rules and are fairly **symmetrical**. Tell students that they will make self-portraits in this activity.

Pass out the materials. Then demonstrate the following procedures as children follow along.

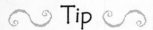

Tip

Have students check the mirror often throughout the drawing process to help them notice individual characteristics and placement of features.

Step by Step

1 Begin with the white paper and pencil. In the center of the paper, draw an egg shape for the face that is a little narrower at the bottom than the top.

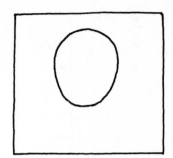

2 Draw the eyes in the middle of the face. The eyes are the shape of a football, tapering to a point on either side. The space in between the eyes can be measured as the width of one eye. Although it is the shape of a circle, the iris is partially covered by the eyelids. Draw two curved sides of the iris. Add a circle for the pupil. It may be helpful for students to think of the shapes and sizes of the eye, iris, and pupil as a football, a softball, and a Ping-Pong ball.

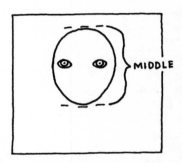

3 Draw eyebrows in an arched shape, indicating the hair with short lines. Draw the upper part of the nose using the side of the pencil. Then gently rub the pencil lines with a fingertip to **shade** the sides of the nose, in between the eyes. Draw a light sketch line halfway between the eyes and the chin to indicate where the nose ends. Use the shading technique for the sides and underneath the nostrils.

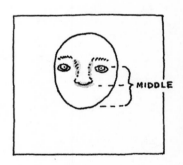

4 Halfway between the nose and the chin, draw a line for the middle of the mouth. Have students notice in the mirror the shape of the upper and lower lips. The upper lip is like a stretched-out letter *M*. The lower lip is a slightly curved line.

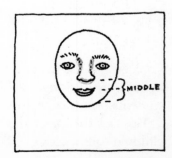

5 Render the ears by making a question mark shape that begins parallel to the eyebrow and ends at the bottom of the nose.

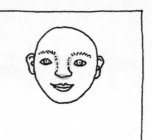

6 Ask students to observe how light makes areas of hair look lighter or darker. Students should notice that whatever color their hair is, it has a variety of shades. This can be indicated with shading and the **blending** of colored pencils. Draw individual strands of hair at the top of the head.

7 Complete the drawing using colored pencils. Encourage students to experiment with mixing and blending colors by **overlapping** and using varying pressure to create light and dark tones.

One Step More

Invite students to write a statement telling what they were thinking at the time they made their self-portraits.

Bookshelf

Looking at Paintings: Children by Peggy Roalf
　　(Hyperion, 1993)
Mary Cassatt by Mike Venezia
　　(Children's Press, 1990)
Picasso by Mike Venezia (Children's Press, 1988)
People by Peter Spier (Doubleday, 1980)
Whoever You Are by Mem Fox
　　(Harcourt Brace, 1997)

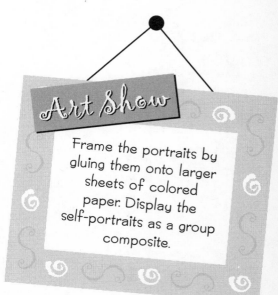

Art Show

Frame the portraits by gluing them onto larger sheets of colored paper. Display the self-portraits as a group composite.

Friends With Hats

In this activity students tip their hats to Pablo Picasso as they paint an imaginary friend with a hat.

Materials

- reproductions of Picasso portraits
- 12- by 18-inch heavy white paper
- pencils
- tempera paint (black, red, yellow, and blue)
- paintbrushes
- water containers
- scissors
- 12- by 18-inch black mounting paper
- glue

New Art Words

abstract

exaggerated

primary colors

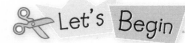 Let's Begin

Introduce the **abstract** portraits by Pablo Picasso. Explain that as the "father of modern art," he helped change the way people look at art. Direct students to look for **exaggerated** facial features and abstract shapes in the portraits.

Pass out the materials. Then demonstrate the following procedures as children follow along.

Step by Step

1 With a pencil, draw a face and shoulders on a sheet of white paper. Suggest that students use the features of a classmate or refer to a magazine photograph for inspiration. Encourage students to use expressive facial features and to add a hat.

Tip

For detailed instructions on drawing a portrait, refer to the self-portrait activity on pages 53–55.

2 Paint large sections of the face, hat, and shoulders using red, blue, and yellow paint. Point out that these bright **primary colors** attract attention to the bold personality in the portrait.

3 Use black paint to outline the facial features. As you work, point out that the shapes begin to look abstract. Pay attention to details such as eyelashes. Use the black paint to invent designs and patterns on the clothing and hat.

4 When the paint is dry, cut out the portrait, leaving a thin white border around the figure. Mount the portraits on black paper.

One Step More

Encourage students to write stories about the people in the portraits they created.

Bookshelf

Picasso: A Day in His Studio by Veronique Antoine (Chelsea House, 1994)

Picasso for Kids by Margaret Hyde (Budding Artists, 1996)

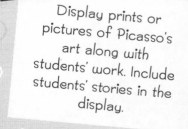

Art Show

Display prints or pictures of Picasso's art along with students' work. Include students' stories in the display.

Symmetrical Smiles

**Students explore symmetry
as they paint bold, abstract
faces in warm and cool colors.**

Materials

- pictures of symmetrical masks or abstract images of faces
- 11- by 17-inch heavy white paper
- pencils
- tempera paint (red, yellow, orange, green, blue, and violet)
- paintbrushes (various sizes)
- water containers
- black crayons
- 12- by 18-inch colored or black construction paper (optional, for mounting)

New Art Words

symmetrical

warm colors

cool colors

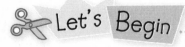 Let's Begin

Have students observe face and mask images and note that a face is the same, or **symmetrical**, on both sides. Draw attention to the geometric shapes (circles, rectangles, squares, and so on) you can use to draw a face. Explain that students will be using these shapes in their own paintings. Point out that some colors convey a feeling of warmth (yellow, orange, and red), whereas others suggest coolness (blue, violet, and green). Use images of the sun and fire as examples of **warm colors** and water and ice for **cool colors** to help students make the connection.

Set up two painting stations, one with warm colors and the other with cool colors. Pass out the materials. Then demonstrate the following procedures as children follow along.

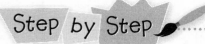

1 Fold a sheet of white paper in half vertically. Draw an *X* anywhere on the fold to indicate which side students should draw on first. Explain to students that they will keep the paper folded and draw only half a face—half a nose, half a mouth, and one eye with one eyebrow.

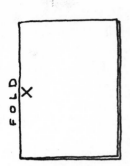

2 Using the look-and-draw method, start halfway from the fold to the outside edge of the paper and draw a geometric shape for the eye. A circle or another shape in the center of the eye can serve as the pupil.

3 Draw half a nose along the fold. The bottom of the nose should end three-quarters of the way down the page.

4 Explain that the shape of the mouth can reflect different moods: upward-facing semicircle—happy, downward-facing semicircle—sad, thin line—anger, and so on. Have students choose an expression and, starting three fingers below the nose (on the fold), draw half a mouth. Suggest that students use geometric shapes for details like eyelashes and cheekbones.

5 Divide the rest of the face with lines, as shown.

Tip

If windows are not available, unfold the paper and refold it with the face on the inside. Begin tracing the face on the side of the paper where there is no drawing (not on the back of the face). When complete, open the paper and trace once again so the face is drawn completely on the full sheet of paper.

6 Trace heavily with pencil over all of the lines drawn to help with the transferring process. Then place the folded paper against a window (blank side facing you) so light shines through the page. Trace over the pencil line. Unfold the paper to see the symmetrical face.

7 Have students paint their faces. Remind them that in order to create symmetrical faces, they must use the same colors on both sides.

8 If desired, use a fine-tipped brush to outline the shapes in black paint, or wait until the painting is completely dry and outline with black crayon.

One Step More

Use yarn or other materials to add details to the faces.

Art Show

Mount the paintings on sheets of black or colored construction paper. Display them as the centerpiece for a bulletin board about symmetry.

Bookshelf

Can You Spot the Leopard? by Fiona Elliot (Prestel, 1997)

Musicians of the Sun by Gerald McDermott (Blue Sky Press, 1994)

Why Mosquitoes Buzz in People's Ears by Verna Aardema (Dial, 1975)

Carnival Creatures

This mask-making project combines social studies with art.

Materials

- pictures of carnival masks
- 12- by 18-inch black construction paper
- light-colored crayons or white chalk
- scissors
- 1-inch-wide strips of fluorescent paper (various lengths)
- white glue
- glitter
- plastic tray or cardboard box
- paper crimper (optional)
- 12- by 18-inch white paper (optional, for mounting)

New Art Words

symmetrical

paper sculpture

fan-folded

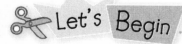

Let's Begin

Tell students that in New Orleans and in South America, Carnival is a celebration at which people wear elaborate and colorful masks and costumes. Explain that in this activity students will create masks from cut paper. Look at masks and costumes from Carnival celebrations to help students gather ideas.

Pass out the materials. Then demonstrate the following procedures as children follow along.

Step by Step

1 Fold a sheet of black paper in half vertically. Have students write an *X* on the side that is faceup to ensure correct drawing placement.

2 Beginning on the fold, about two inches down from the top of the paper, guide students through a look-and-draw outline of the mask. (Have them use light-colored crayons or white chalk so that it shows up on the black paper.) Tell students that their mask outlines can include lines for hair and ears; they may also use points, curves, and other shapes. Instruct students to draw to the outside edges of the paper and end at the bottom of the fold.

3 Draw an eye shape toward the top of the page. Bend this area and snip with scissors. Cut out the eye shape.

4 With the paper still folded, cut out the mask along the drawn line. The mask will be **symmetrical**.

5 Use the paper strips to add a nose, mouth, eyebrows, and other ornamentation to the mask in a symmetrical pattern. **Paper sculpture** can include **fan-folded** pieces, curled strips, and any other sculptured pieces that students want to create.

6 Highlight selected areas with white glue and add glitter for a special carnival effect.

~ **Tip** ~

To avoid a mess, use a plastic tray or cardboard box to collect the glitter.

 One Step More

A paper crimper adds a great texture to the paper strips. Students may use the crimper on their own, or you might have crimped strips ready for use.

Art Show

Mount the completed carnival masks on white paper and display by clipping to a clothesline strung across the room.

Bookshelf

Celebrate in Central America by Joe Viesti and Diane Hall (Lothrop, Lee & Shepard, 1997)

Festivals: Carnival by Clare Chandler (Millbrook Press, 1998)

Festivals of the World: Brazil by Susan McKay (Gareth Stevens, 1997)

Tonight Is Carnival by Arthur Dorros (Dutton, 1995)

Beach Ball Collage

This project taps into summer memories and teaches students about the color wheel and collage techniques.

Materials

- color wheel pattern (see page 67)
- umbrella and blanket patterns (see page 68)
- crayons
- scissors
- 12- by 18-inch tagboard
- glue
- craft sticks
- pencils
- watercolor paints
- paintbrushes
- water containers
- sand or fine sawdust (optional)

New Art Words

texture
color wheel
primary colors
secondary colors
composition
color spectrum

Let's Begin

Begin with a discussion of things that people take to the beach, including beach balls, plastic toys, umbrellas, sand pails, and shovels. Talk about things people enjoy about the beach, such as water, sand, and sun. Talk about **texture**—how the sand feels: smooth, coarse, soft, and so on. Ask students to describe what they see on a beach ball (usually several sections of color). Then introduce the **color wheel**, explaining that the **primary colors**, red, yellow, and blue, are mixed together to form the **secondary colors**, orange, green, and violet.

Duplicate the patterns on pages 67–68 so that each student has a copy. Pass out the other materials. Then demonstrate the following procedures.

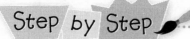

Step by Step

1 Begin by explaining that a **composition** is a pleasing arrangement of objects in a picture or painting. Explain that students will create a beach picture that will include a beach ball, blanket, umbrella, and sand pail with shovel. Help students plan where they will place the ball and sand pail. Explain that students will add the umbrella last but should be sure to leave room for it.

2 To create a color wheel, color the top section with red crayon. Move clockwise and add orange, yellow, green, blue, and violet in that order. Discuss with the class that in the **color spectrum**, red and yellow mix to create orange, yellow and blue mix to create green, and blue and red mix to create violet.

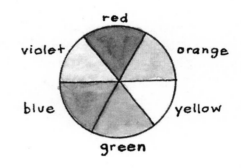

3 Cut out the color wheel and glue it onto the bottom of the tagboard. Explain that the color wheel is a beach ball.

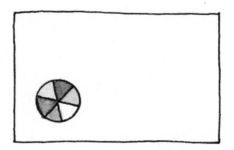

4 Color the blanket and umbrella stripes in the same order of primary and secondary colors used on the ball.

5 Have students cut out and place the umbrella shape and blanket on the tagboard near the ball. Glue the craft stick in place for the umbrella handle, and then glue the umbrella top and blanket onto the tagboard.

6 Use the look-and-draw method to add the sand pail to another spot on the tagboard. Encourage students to choose their own spot rather than copy yours exactly. Add lines to form six sections. Draw a handle and shovel.

7 Color the sand pail in the same order as the ball.

8 Use watercolors to paint the sky.

9 Using a mixture of water and white glue, brush over the sand area. (Do not try to do all of it at once.) Sprinkle the glued area with sand or fine sawdust. Textured coloring may be used if sand or sawdust is not available. Lay a rough surface under the paper, and using the side of a crayon, rub over it to give it texture.

One Step More

After the artwork is dry, have students add several seagulls to the scene. Tell students that professional artists usually paint odd numbers of birds.

Art Show

Display the beach scenes on a beach towel stapled to a bulletin board in the hallway. Also display several beach items if you have them on hand.

Bookshelf

At the Beach With Dad by Mercer Mayer (Inchworm Press, 1998)

Beach Bunny by Jennifer Selby (Harcourt Brace, 1996)

Beach Play by Marsha Hayles (Henry Holt, 1998)

Lottie's New Beach Towel by Petra Mathers (Atheneum, 1998)

Color Wheel Pattern

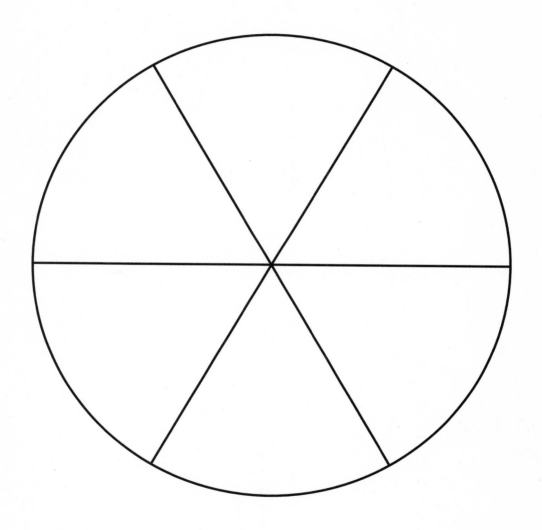

Umbrella and Blanket Patterns

Art Projects That Dazzle & Delight: Grades 2–3 Scholastic Professional Books

Geometric Fish

**Geometry, science,
and art all work together
as students create
colorful paper fish.**

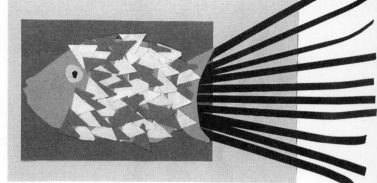

Materials

- pictures of fish
- 9- by 12-inch construction paper (various colors)
- pencils
- scissors
- glue sticks
- markers
- precut construction paper triangles (various colors)
- 12- by 18-inch construction paper (various colors)
- 1/4- by 6-inch black construction paper strips (optional)

*New Art
Word*

triangular

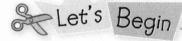 Let's Begin

Show students pictures of a variety of fish, and have them look for
different shapes and colors. Explain that students will create cut paper
fish using different shapes and colors.

Pass out the materials. Then demonstrate the following procedures as
children follow along.

Step by Step

1 Fold a sheet of 9- by 12-inch paper in half vertically. Draw an *X* about 1 inch from the top and another *X* 3 to 4 inches from the bottom on the fold line. Tell students that this indicates where the fish's body will begin and end.

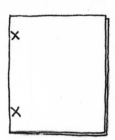

2 With pencil draw half of a large oval beginning at one *X* and ending at the other. Cut out the fish shape and save the remaining scraps to create the tail.

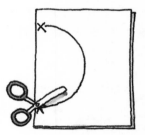

3 Choose another color of 9- by 12-inch paper and glue the fish onto it.

4 To create the tail, use the largest scrap of paper left over from the body. Keeping the paper folded, draw a curved line almost to the top edge of the paper. Return the line (keeping it curved to match the other) to the fold of the paper. Cut out the tail shape and glue it onto one end of the body.

5 To add lips, cut out a circle from the scrap paper and then cut it in half. Glue the halves one above the other, as shown.

6 Use the precut paper triangles for the scales. Starting near the tail, draw a line of glue from the top of the fish to the bottom. Press the **triangular** shapes onto the glue line from top to bottom, overlapping slightly. When the first row is complete, follow the same procedure to continue overlapping each row slightly. Rows should go one-half to three-quarters of the way down the fish. Leave room for the eye.

7 To make the eye, cut out a circle from a scrap of different-colored paper. A smaller black circle may be added in the middle for the pupil. Your fish is now complete.

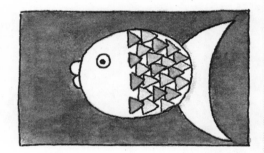

~ ⚬ Tip ⚬ ~

Add strips of black construction paper to the tail to make it a fanciful fantail fish. Strips should be approximately 1/4 inch in width and 6 to 8 inches long.

One Step More

Glue the entire fish onto a sheet of 12- by 18-inch construction paper of a different color. Then glue black paper strips to the tail so that they extend off the page.

Art Show

Cover a wall or bulletin board with blue craft paper and place the fish on it to create a classroom aquarium.

Bookshelf

Fish Eyes: A Book You Can Count On
  by Lois Ehlert (Harcourt Brace, 1990)

Fish Is Fish by Leo Lionni (Pantheon, 1970)

The Rainbow Fish by Marcus Pfister
  (North-South Books, 1992)

Swimmy by Leo Lionni (Knopf, 1963)

Weaving Water Creatures

In this activity students "weave together" creatures of the sea.

Materials

- pictures of ocean life
- fish and turtle patterns (pages 75–76)
- 9- by 12-inch construction paper (warm and cool colors, and black)
- rulers
- pencils
- scissors
- 1- by 9-inch strips of construction paper in warm and cool colors
- glue

New Art Words

warm colors

cool colors

color scheme

weaving

Let's Begin

Introduce the idea that colors often reflect feelings. Familiar expressions such as "I feel blue" or "looking at the world through rose-colored glasses" are just two examples. Review the **warm colors** (yellow, red, and orange) and the **cool colors** (blue, purple, and green). Tell students that they will use either a cool or a warm **color scheme** to create a sea creature. Explain that this is a **weaving** project. Display and discuss ocean life pictures for inspiration.

Reproduce the patterns on pages 75–76. Let students choose one for their project and have them cut it out. Pass out the other materials. Then demonstrate the following procedures.

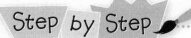

1 Have students select a sheet of colored paper. Fold the sheet in half horizontally. Using a ruler placed on the open edge, draw a line along the edge of the ruler from side to side. This is the "Stop" line. (It may help to have students write "Stop" on this line.)

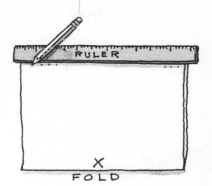

2 Have students place an *X* on the folded edge. Instruct them to keep the folded edge near their body and the open edge away from it. (It is crucial for success that students cut on the folded edge!) Using the width of the ruler, draw a line from the top of the folded edge to the "stop" line. Moving the ruler, continue drawing lines until you run out of space.

3 On the folded edge with the *X*, begin cutting the lines until you reach the "Stop" line. Continue until all lines have been cut.

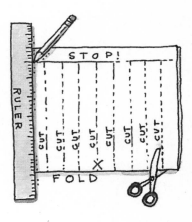

4 Open up the folded paper. Choose strips of paper in the same warm or cool color family as the base paper. Weave a strip in an over-and-under motion through the cut base paper. Continue weaving with other strips, using an alternating color pattern and pushing the strips as close together as possible for stability and strength.

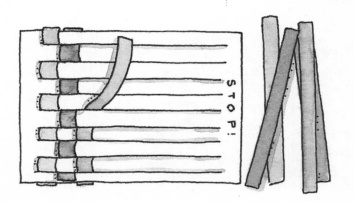

5 On a sheet of colored or black paper, trace the fish or sea turtle pattern. (It must not touch the edge of the paper.) To cut out this shape, demonstrate how to make a small hole in the middle of the shape to insert scissors. Then cut to the outline of the shape to make a frame. Cut out bubbles, if desired. This frame will then be glued on top of the weaving.

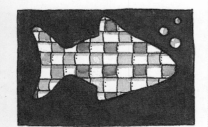

6 On the frame, place a thin line of glue along the edge of the cutout shape. Then place a thin line of glue along the outside edge of the frame. Carefully place this paper on top of the woven paper and press down.

One Step More

Before students glue the frame in place, encourage them to cut out ocean motifs—simple shapes such as starfish, shells, seaweed, and smaller fish. Or students can cut these from the scraps of colored paper. Have students glue these onto the corners of their frame.

Bookshelf

Coral Reef Fishes by Ewald Lieske
   (Princeton University Press, 1996)

Fish Eyes: A Book You Can Count On by Lois Ehlert
   (Harcourt Brace, 1990)

The National Audubon Society Field Guide to North American Fishes, Whales and Dolphins by H. Boschung, J. Williams, D. Gotshall, D. Caldwell, M. Caldwell (Alfred A. Knopf, 1983)

One Fish Two Fish Red Fish Blue Fish by Dr. Seuss
   (Random House, 1960)

Origami Sea Life by John Montoll (Dover, 1991)

Swimmy by Leo Lionni (Pantheon, 1963)

What Is a Fish? by David Eastman (Troll, 1982)

Art Show

Display these ocean creatures on a bulletin board with crepe paper twirled to resemble seaweed.

Fish Pattern

Sea Turtle
Pattern

Art Projects That Dazzle & Delight: Grades 2–3   Scholastic Professional Books

Rainbow of Butterflies

Students work with the colors of the spectrum to create rainbows framed by a butterfly silhouette.

Materials

- butterfly wing pattern (page 80)
- scissors
- 12- by 18-inch heavy white paper
- pencils
- tempera paint (red, blue, and yellow)
- easel brushes
- trays for mixing colors
- water containers
- pictures of butterflies
- 12- by 18-inch black paper
- white pencil or crayon
- glue

New Art Words

ROY G. BIV

spectrum

primary colors

secondary colors

symmetry

✂ Let's Begin

Discuss the colors in a rainbow. Ask students if they know who was named after the rainbow. Introduce **ROY G. BIV**, and explain that the letters in his name represent the first letters of the colors in the **spectrum** (red, orange, yellow, green, blue, indigo, and violet). Tell students that they will be mixing **primary colors** (red, yellow, and blue) to create **secondary colors** (green, orange, and violet). They will not use indigo.

Duplicate the butterfly pattern on page 80 so that each student has one. Have children cut out the butterfly pattern along the outside edge. Pass out the other materials and demonstrate the following procedures as children follow along.

Step by Step

1 Divide a sheet of white paper into six painting sections. Fold the paper in half horizontally to crease a center line. Using a pencil, draw two lines above the crease and two lines below it to create six sections, approximately two inches in height each. Label each space with one letter of ROY G. BV, as shown.

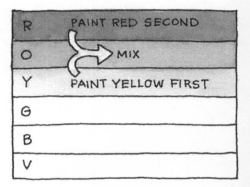

2 Paint in the space marked *Y* with yellow paint. Use a smooth, continuous brushstroke. Paint in the *R* space with red paint. Mix the red paint on the brush with a portion of the yellow in the tray or directly on the paper to create the secondary color orange. Paint in the *O* space with orange paint.

3 Rinse the paintbrush, and paint the remaining spaces in the same way. Mix blue with yellow to create green. Mix blue with red to create violet. The entire paper should be filled with color. Let the papers dry overnight.

4 Display colorful butterfly pictures. Draw students' attention to the **symmetry** of butterfly wings. Guide students to examine black outlines in the patterns of the wings.

5 Fold the black paper in half vertically. Use a white pencil or crayon to trace the butterfly wing pattern.

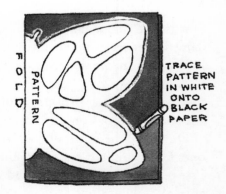

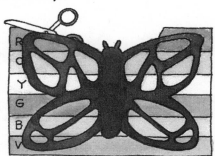

6 Keep the paper folded and draw six large shapes inside the wings. These shapes must not touch. (Use the pattern as a model.)

7 Keep the paper folded. Use a pencil to punch a small hole in the center of each shape on the wing. Push the scissors through the holes to make a clean cut. Be sure to cut through top and bottom layers at the same time. This will create symmetry in the butterfly. With the paper still folded, cut along the outside of the butterfly.

8 Open the butterfly and place it on the painted rainbow paper. For a neat, finished look, glue the penciled side onto the paper. Trim away painted paper edges.

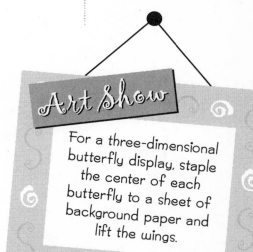

Tip

Glue the center of the butterfly first. It is easier to lift the sides to apply more glue.

One Step More

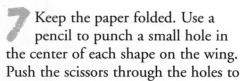

Use pipe cleaners or scraps of black paper for antennae.

Bookshelf

A Bad Case of Stripes by David Shannon (Scholastic, 1998)

Butterflies by John Wexo (Zoo Books, 1993)

The Butterfly Hunt by Yoshi (Picture Book Studio, 1990)

From Caterpillar to Butterfly by Deborah Heiligman (HarperCollins, 1996)

Art Show

For a three-dimensional butterfly display, staple the center of each butterfly to a sheet of background paper and lift the wings.

Butterfly Wing Pattern

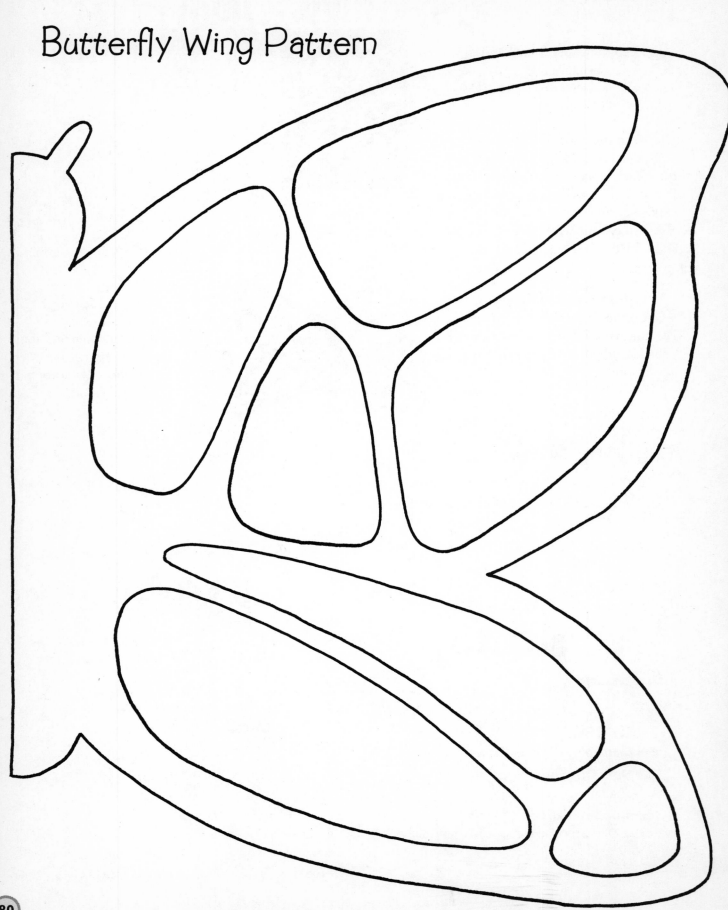

Art Projects That Dazzle & Delight: Grades 2–3   Scholastic Professional Books